Tom's Fishing Day

Yvonne Smith

Illustrated by Ron Wheeler

Copyright © 2023 Yvonne Smith

Copyright © 2023 TEACH Services, Inc.

ISBN-13: 978-1-4796-1467-7 (Paperback)

ISBN-13: 978-1-4796-1468-4 (ePub)

Library of Congress Control Number: 2023904837

TEACH Services, Inc.
P U B L I S H I N G
www.TEACHServices.com • (800) 367-1844

It was Tom's birthday. The sun shone brightly through his bedroom window. He knew that it was going to be a beautiful day for him to go fishing.

He rubbed his eyes as the sun beamed brightly into them. He smiled happily. It was his fourth birthday.

Dad walked into Tom's bedroom, feeling very happy himself. He, too, was waiting for this special day.

"Are you sleeping, Son?" Lifting Tom up into his arms, he held him close and hugged him.

"Happy birthday! Are you ready for your trip?" Dad asked. Tom smiled more beautifully than the sunshine that was coming through his window. "Why not, Dad? It is my birthday. I have been waiting so long, and it is finally here." "Well, let us get ready, Tom."

They got dressed. Tom took his
fishing hook and
a small basket.

They got into the truck,
and they were on their
journey to the pond.

"We are here, Dad. Where are the fish?"

Dad smiled at Tom. "You won't see the fish, Tom. You will have to put your hook down into the water. Come over here and hand me the hook."

Tom watched his dad as he let down the hook into the water.

"Hold this, Tom, here."

Tom held the hook nervously as his dad showed him how to fish. "When you feel a tug on the hook, pull."

Tom looked at his dad and watched eagerly as he let down his hook into the water. "Did you catch any fish, Dad?"

"No," Dad replied. "I will have to try again. It's your turn, Tom. Now you try."

Tom was very excited. "This is awesome," Tom said as he let down his hook into the water.

"I will sit here and watch you, Tom, as you fish."

"Dad, I will be lucky this time."
Dad nodded his head as he watched Tom let down his hook into the water. Suddenly, Tom felt a pull on his hook. He pulled it quickly from the water.

"Dad! Dad! Dad! Look! Wow! I caught a big fish. I caught it all by myself. Dad, I caught it all by myself! Come and help me pull it from the hook."

Dad was very pleased. He was very happy, too. "Good job, son." He patted Tom on his shoulder.

"This will be your birthday dinner. Mom will prepare it for us. She will be proud of you too, Tom."

"Dad, I do not want Mom to cook it yet. I want all my friends to see what I caught on my fourth birthday."

"Okay, I will let all of your friends and everybody in the family see your fish, Tom," Dad said.

Tom was so proud of himself. Later that evening, he told all his friends and his mom all about his fishing lesson.

"I can't wait for my friends and family to see my big fish," he said as he stared at the fish. "I can't wait for my next birthday!" he exclaimed as he hugged his mom.

"I wonder what Dad will teach me next."

"Here, Tom." Dad gave him a fishing net. "Use this on your next trip, Tom," Dad said, with a smile on his face. "Dad, I am only four, and I can fish. Thank you, Dad!"

Dad reminded Tom about the call by the sea in Matthew 4:18–22 of the disciples who were fishing all night and did not catch any fish.

However, with Jesus' presence and command, they were able to catch fish. "They caught a net full of fish that night," he told Tom. He reminded Tom that Christ gave him the knowledge and the ability to fish, and that's why he could teach Tom how to fish. Looking upon his dad's face in amazement, Tom held on to his dad's hand.

"Let us promise God to say a little prayer each time we catch a fish from now on," he said. Dad held on tightly to Tom's hand and said, "Let us do it now." Dad and Tom bowed their heads.

"Thank You, God, for Tom and for the wisdom You have given me to apply knowledge. Thank You for making my little boy happy on his birthday and allowing him to catch this big fish that could bring glory to You and more joy to his heart, Amen."

TEACH Services, Inc.
P U B L I S H I N G

We invite you to view the complete
selection of titles we publish at:
www.TEACHServices.com

We encourage you to write us
with your thoughts about this,
or any other book we publish at:
info@TEACHServices.com

TEACH Services' titles may be purchased in
bulk quantities for educational, fund-raising,
business, or promotional use.
bulksales@TEACHServices.com

Finally, if you are interested in seeing
your own book in print, please contact us at:
publishing@TEACHServices.com
We are happy to review your manuscript at no charge.

www.ingramcontent.com/pod-product-compliance
Lightning Source LLC
Chambersburg PA
CBHW061417090426
42742CB00026B/3493